Hagiography

Jen Currin

Coach House Books | Toronto

Canada Council   Conseil des Arts
for the Arts   du Canada
 ONTARIO ARTS COUNCIL
CONSEIL DES ARTS DE L'ONTARIO
Canadä

Published with the generous assistance of the Canada Council
for the Arts and the Ontario Arts Council. Coach House Books
also acknowledges the support of the Government of Ontario
through the Ontario Book Publishing Tax Credit and the
Government of Canada through the Book Publishing Industry
Development Program.

LIBRARY AND ARCHIVES CANADA CATALOGUING IN PUBLICATION

Currin, Jen, 1972-
Hagiography / Jen Currin.

Poems.
ISBN 978-1-55245-197-7

I. Title.

PS8605.U77H34 2008   C811'.6   C2008-900669-0

For my beloveds

TABLE OF CONTENTS

DEATH

INTERMISSION

CHILDHOOD

INTERMISSION

BIRTH

DEATH

CHANTING INDOORS

For the fish are drunk again
in the streets of your city.
It can be hard to find a ring
for every finger.
With the beads and the counting and the indoors.
With the mountain at the back gate.
And where to house the glass star.

It happens in myth
every time a woman looks over her shoulder.
She wants lunch. Points to her elbow.
First salt then boiling water.
Demons soaked in the sink.
It happens wherever we are silent.

For a pilgrim needs water. Weariness.
Two fish saved in a jug.
The pilgrim is a body
poured from cup to mouth.
In the end it will be as when we first shook hands.
Fires near the city.
The mayor rinses her vest.
We look at our legs and ask will they save us.

LYRIC

Your friend and his brothers of coastal address
don't look good on paper.
In every corner a ghost
falling to its knees,
too much hope at the mouth.
They study English desperately
but won't remove their shoes.

This is being light.
The best light we can find.
A woman gives a man
her intuition.
He pockets it in a game
called Pass the First Jewel on Your Left.
And your friends, the whites
of their eyes are blue.
They make our nipples into poems
in neighbourhoods where coffee is roasted.

Even when we are naked
lions caught in traffic,
we stupidly split our lips
remembering.
A woman kills a man
and he becomes a piano.
The next time we meet
it will be too romantic,
just a few words and a thousand
intricately carved boxes.
Let us breathe into them
until we are dead.

I asked to follow the thread and you said,
Have faith and drink water.
Leaning on your language,
I forgot my luggage:
pictures of a many-tiered virginity,
unlikable characters, their battered shoes.

Each tree had to be thanked
so I set to my task.
Some of the spirits were eating candy,
some had apocalyptic faces.
They asked after my bags,
if my brother had given me vitamins.

Dogs named after our distant relatives
dropped bones at my feet.
The spirits urged me to hold up a branch
and act like a magician
but I refused.
Since birth I have been afraid of stories.

It was my mother
who took the oranges to the border,
argued with the guards.
She made appearances in cash only.

We woke frenzied, unable to spell.
It fell from our mouths: *We are bridges.*
More and more of us resonate.
I can't remember, but I'm sure it was you
who finally told me
it doesn't matter if we run toward it
or run away.

It can be had
by friends adult and elderly.
Lonely – a finger without a ring.
In the depths of sobriety
I'm hiding the string
we use to discern a woman's character.
A train platform in the middle of nowhere.

Travelling south with a bag of licorice,
a tea jar from Japan.
The city is always late and missing
its panties. It's best to pretend
we don't know why.
I don't want you to ever lie
next to someone and not touch her
because of me.
In the dark you have to trust
the stairs.

To be tall and naked
as a tree. Transient –
we've already seen the bones.
Two fish cradling the family.
Two sisters and I am
one of them.

Death speaks like a feather: yellow.
Green: death's mountain at the foot of your youth.
Red: assume death.
Love: too many poems death would rather forget.
Love: just like a little storm it topples,
making a name for itself.
River: not a thin blanket,
never a narrow
pair of shoes.
Laughter: spilled passport.
Knock: down.
The silver: walls.
If death is speaking
(sunset: specific: pleasant clock)
I'd like it to get to the point:
the boys running into the house
for her glasses.
Later she never wore them
and claimed it was our wish.
Black: as she remembers.
Tremor: you'd think it was her coffin.
Lilacs: where the old kings
are sleeping I heard
eleven ring twice.

A practice of breaking night
over your knee, never lifting
a finger in the larger struggle.

New arrivals lurk outside the candle's circle.
My clinic is full of intelligent people.
My husband pregnant and no memory.
For facial hair
I use coffee grounds.
The world is very tender;
we are a village together.

Now the tongue our parents spoke of
is proof we are decaying.
Piece together the sweaty children
and you have a concern.
Not really outraged, words
clipped like wings.
We are in a fire of intelligent people
and not one knows

even the word *cup* will disappear.

THE BLOOD WE MEDITATE

Every sister knows the rats.
A salad to be shared
in the rented kitchen.

Her intent is to be sick in her shoes
and then walk home.
Never to grow and never to be scorned.
For the sun is distant from our table.

We buy a book of propaganda.
A prop horse from a man in robes.
His concern is our lack of.
Are we in town for a while.
Would we like a free meal.

By betrayal, I mean the waterfall
crying behind us.
Our sides ache from laughing.
How better to deface ourselves.
Surely we are pigeons
performing in the war theatre.
Surely the man will publish
his accusatory drawings.
He wants the colour of our eyes,
our hairy vision.
How strange he wants the wind
to forget us –

IT SEEMS

Dear Death,
please tell me it was you
dressed as a dancing girl
listening at the door.
I'm sorry my sisters
whispered so softly.
They had just begun to disappear
like snow on the lower mountains.

I'm sad you're not someone else,
but who is.
My parents have been skeletons for years.
There's nothing to be ashamed of.

I have three pairs of pants
with which to drive out the moonlight.
I will leave them at the port
for your seamstress.

If you return me to the seasons
with new claws, I will not remember this
crime. I will wake slowly
as a bee drowns in my coffee.

Dear Death, it is already yesterday
as we board your blue boat.

SHADOW/DISTINCTION

Boys of the frog illiterate
lighten our studies
in the man-woman-tiger church.

A willingness to be ourselves –
of little value,
carved from the lap of a god.

Something in their eye. Some man in our ear.
A year from youth
choking on good advice.

We will recognize
their teeth, miserable setting
for a play.

Our fathers dead in the kitchen,
the musicians fighting
in alley tongue.

Light at eight
in April, pigeons grooming
by some other clock.

Someone veiled, weeping
over a homemade broom.

Pulse of a wrist –
another entrance.

CONSTELLATIONS, CREATURES WITH TWO LEGS

Bluish in the whiskered face of dawn,
I lift my cloak to the sky –
face after farce – April's marriage
to August. My love who was
the size of a thumb. Bottled
and given to idle phrase-making.
A phantom in a noisy place
before her army slowed its pace.

Now a mermaid tattoo, a blue monkey, a bird
frightened by chance,
seeing a black squirrel
in the car's shadow. Dogs on film
and no one wants to hold her hand
in exile.

Inscrutably involved, your hands are basil.
You fall into a fugue that could be a garden.
Once upon a forest I cut myself
and claimed I was the knife.
My love who knew the taste of mountains.
Red clover tea. Kiss on the knee.

Sickness was the star sitting too close
on the divan. Vanity sipping the baffled waters.
The dead and living waters
we pour over our heads. Our shoulders
brush. Our spirits will not
marry us.

TOPPLE THE ROOM

We think madness is green and we are yellow.
Shown sideways, our scars gleam
their first warnings
as we go next door with our heartbeats,
our handfuls of rice.

The whole house smells of burning.
It is not the time for headstands yet.
I cannot ask
the you of yesterday
to be the you of today,
for I too once spiked my hair
to appear worthy.

For we lived in a thicket,
sleeping back to back
as if married.
Maybe I am sick but I return
to this as if it will never go out.
Night after night,
in the dead light of my blood's
poorest translation,
I dream in our name.

FINALLY, WHO IS HERE WITH US?

A man hits his granddaughter with a sock.
We are sinking deeper into the muck.
I stand on one foot like a duck.
All the cats follow me
across the gravel like sugar thieves.

So the wire bird abandons writing.
I give up
my plastic mouse.
The apartment lobby choked with incense,
red leaves piled at the door.
A donkey who loves to drink wine.
A little piece of yellow paper
for your mother on the Sunshine Coast.

I keep falling off the table. What do I know.
Erotic ideals. Orange and a slice of pie.
What do I know. The sun leaves me.
All the children I know are me.

In the desert we go barefoot and pregnant.

Finally, we reach the seventh day.

Finally, we reach the eighth sister.

Silence, I wish you sounded more like rain.

WE ALL DRIVE SUCH CARS

No longer myself sing breathlessly
with force short of war.
I picked up a small lisp in that other country.
Lowercase conversations, paragraphs of horses –
it disappoints me
that I see you so rarely.

For days longer we may linger
in doorways, democratically wishing,
indiscriminately locking bicycles to poles.

You use the word *path* four times
in one sentence. Why?

I am resting, really.
Wearing the garden in my hat,
I promise to make it briefly ours.
Floors everywhere remind me
of your back. Mountainous night,
cats let loose in the lobby.

You once pinched the balcony,
tossed it to the rocks.
Such silences poured over,
had nothing to do with me.
We are all named
after a place
we once lived and I refuse
to weave a part in this biography.
Brutality taught me:
leaf is a verb.
I am leaving.

THE ELEPHANT LADY'S DRAWINGS

We came out of the garden
and there were brides in the trees.
You faked a birdsong.
I had something to say to your mother
but the ancestors are as inconsiderate
as they are deaf.

To the house of sliding panels
we rode optimistically
side by side, downing
the vinegary local wine.
Our anxious friends
had become famous.
Some favoured men; others, women.
They set our places at the table.

It was like a dream of masturbation:
you dipping the artichoke in melted butter.
I wanted to drool
if that was what it meant to be wild,
but I could only comfort you
as you comforted the wall.

Don't close my eyes when I die.
I want my body rubbed
with white sand, the strongest teas
imbibed at my grave.
I can settle for little:
a calmness after crying,
honey for the throat.
Because my list is endless —

to dream of pigs,
good-luck animals advancing
like territories of water and ash.
These tender people in the light of their deaths
studying to protect you
like gold through your nose.
They read the book
from its end
to its beginning.

You call to the money, always small
as your friends. From under
your pseudonym, the festival:
butterfly meets butterfly
on the highway median.
A word taken
up and down until our jackets
are left hanging
in whisper-hands.

Very much like the white bird
you saw me and gave me free
your wooded message –

Who used to bring me milk
before the war.

TO SHRINK THE RIVER

The ghost chokes
on teeth,
I am hesitant
to make a home
for it.

The cake turning to mountain
in the ghost's stomach.
To fold an egg into bed.
To take a pill,
blue as it should be.
To make the names
dance hypnotically
in their cribs.

Winter aghast, joining
our howls
in the churning river.
Noise only you notice
as I hoarsely wish
for a place
in the death tank,
shortest day
out of my mouth
like an anonymous egg.

IF WE ARE ABLE

All night and again
in the morning.
The shorter   the shortest   breath.
I will listen
with my whole body
while we are still alive.

A flesh and bone house.
A muscle house.
Some still, selfish door.
The snow country of your shirt,
a candle burning invisibly
at midday.

                    *

One snake, an eye
at the back of your head.
Three trees, a forest
where the offspring are divided
young from old.

They bring in a cousin
or an aunt to cry,
but no torture.
They deprive us of sleep,
but no torture.
Only a shower
of rice. And we must
say something now
about how hard it is.

OFTEN AT NIGHT, OFTEN WITH CANDLES

In a jar with my
                hush money.

Bomb where I live.

Two ways of saying
                intimacy.

If suicide.

If you believe in one small luck.

Only women with the gold pig pendant.

What do they mean to do
with their predictions.

Heavy   eye   mouth   ear.

Nine months out
                of the year.

Where the good
                spirits live.

                                How will they.

Little brothers with their bowls
at the window.
In skirts, in pockets
of ash.

THE BRIDGE MELTING BEHIND US

Give until the glass
is empty, until the sky is salt,
until the self disowns
the self. Give like the wind
and forget what you touch.

And please burn your owls
out of their habits.
Feathers beget eggs.
I want to tell you this
on a piece of onion skin:
you always look bigger standing
in the doorway.

We walk to where tomorrow preens.
Wind-demons belly dance on the bridge.
The gulls make quick confetti
of our words.
Let us say the most shocking thing.

My dear husband/wife, I want to tell you now,
as you are both sleeping beside me
and working on your novel
in the next room. All these years,
I have not been a human being.
All these years I have been a tree.

Deep breath to begin the sexual pause. A patient grasp on the sentence. Trees let go. They have to. Lean in. As wishbones do. Intact on the windowsill. Wings in our teeth. Breast to breast. We will marry in burnt swaddling clothes. Let it be known in the city of our distraction. In debt like the moon. The phone's celestial ringing. The piano hushed. Polishing the paragraph of bone. Over breakfasts of blood pastries. We shower in dust. Tune of red ants. If we sleep through the war and wake to find no one.

INTERMISSION

She had the look of winter about her. An inexhaustible redness to her breast. Hunger in the shape of an eye. Crest like a bony crown.

It's bad luck to give an even number of flowers. Here are thirteen daffodils. I'd like you to come back, so please leave your face in the mirror by the front door.

I'm not afraid of your nursery-rhyme demons. But who will supply the bath amulets? Some little fellow from the wood stopped me yesterday near his house. *See that bird?* he asked. *See that wizard?*

ACROBATS GLOW IN THE DARK

If I bend you this way,
you curl like a fiddlehead.
If you twist me quickly, sirens
break.

The mountain raises its shoulder
like an eyebrow. Is not shocked
by our grooming. How we take
a comb to bed and tell
a lover to leave
her pants on the floor
so we may sweep the spirits
from the apartment.

A colony of small red spiders
eats their queen. You cannot domesticate
these plants. The palm drops its fronds
and leaves us with an erection.
We buy shorter legs
for the couch.
We bide our time on a mattress
on the floor.

The halls smell of cumin.
The carnival is a block away.
The brothel where we clip our fingernails
when we are in the mood.

WINDOW MUSIC

Because the red bird says it will know me
if I put a fish whistle in my pocket.
It's like laughter how we catch our breath.
Like laughter at three
in the morning.

So I set down my skin. I'm tired.
There is a wall on either side.
A safety pin for an earring.
A lover who picks tomatoes for the ride.

The ceiling drops its plants to the floor.
Dust from the other room.
Drinking paper and brown rice tea.
Drinking gold and olive oil.
I'm seeing stars on the stair.

I doff my cap to the trees.
I drop my list
and start over.

A peach is eaten
while leaning against brick.
Soon I will recognize the sun.

NO ONE NEED KNOW WE'RE NOT HOME

We take the first steps to the sea.
A paper bride blows by.
You write a note on my hand
and ask me who wrote it.

Penny-eyed, the seals accuse us.
We have left their brothers
in the bath. We have left
the lights on in the spice cupboard.

And now the ocean's broken laughter.
I pull the instructions
from a small hourglass.
My gloves are stiff with salt,
every finger a hot stone.

*

More than once we have been eaten
by the sea. The wind whistles *dumber, smarter*.
A bit of foam clings to your forehead.
The wind guesses who a flower, who a leaf.

*

You are spinning, your red pyjamas
bunched at the ankles, your spirit
napping in the old nursery.

My shoes turn to seaweed.
The wind forces me to my knees.
I swiftly learn how to crawl.
A shred of a tune tumbles
down the beach like a jailbird kite.

Threads of the sweater I threw away last year
have found their way into your hair.
We go from green to blue to green again,
unable to make up our minds.

EATING THE SCRAPS OF DAWN

You take off your powder
and come to know me
as I am,
stairs into water and the sun
in your eyes.

Of all the criers you comfort me most.
You are the only one who takes me for a madman,
who understands my throat
thinks for me.

October sidles up. We've been eating phantom money.
And you? Wet haired in your bed.
And you? Smoking in the snow.
We've been up this mountain before, bleeding,
thank you for asking.

Still I like the buildings and I still hope
to make a friend from the encounter
before the sky does.
I age much. It must seem
that I like to look over my shoulder.
I'm not so indiscriminate as all that.

THE MOUNTAIN HIGHWAY

My beggar's spirit and I are one.
We agree to leave
in the morning.
About the time the road begins to whine,
I remember the bottle hidden in the blankets.
We can't turn back to the year of the dragon
where two treed men
might drop their webs over us,
so we brave the winding path
to the city of blood dancers.
We eat nothing, sing to the small dog
that might be a phantom.
A blossom in the room of my mind wilts slowly.
I cannot remember which coin
is our talisman.
Near the city gates, we join a masked procession
of incarcerated gods.
There is a small chance
we too will end up whistling.

FORTUNES FOR A TWO-BEARDED WOMAN

First lick two envelopes. Leave them
unsealed. Then begin mending:
shirts, shoes, pants. Quietly. Merrily.
Fill up the space between your fingers
with hoarse song.

There is a peasant army hiding
in the fig tree and the path is overgrown
with morning glory.
Masked damsels say *bird*, say *rifle*.
Blood sleeps in their beds.
Say *knife*. Say *spoon*.

It is not raining yet
on this side of town.
The train stretches lonesome across the bridge.
A bruised hat falls to the water.
The bell of a belt buckle as it hits
the rocks.

If your father gives you
ten thousand dancing girls,
you will dress as a sailor
in an archipelago of tattoos.
If you sew a button
on your brown suit,
you will not envy the orchid.
You will notice the crescent
of your lover's body curled in sleep.
You will read this with both of your hands.

CHILDHOOD

RUMOURS AND TREMBLING

I tell the teeth of your mouth:
I waited for you
and the devil never came.
Now he misses the rain,
whistles in the night
to become the snake
in spy photographs.

Just as we use fish bones
to fortune tell,
he holds up his trousers
with no hands.
We are all capable of this,
having spent our whole lives
questioning birds.

Drawing circles in the sky.
Catching matches
when our arms are long.
We lose getting lost
at the end of the day.

It could be lonely, a bed
of blue roses
over the mountains.

Your shoes get too tight,
you forget, and the truth
as we know it
is worn away.

CHILDHOOD

Kindling I laid down on as you stole my fast. We ate masks of lamb bones and sweet grasses. Then I threw my hair on the ground and would go no further.

Belly down, you listened as the newly tarred road turned to snake. I had two eyes at the time and I told you to get the hell inside. The sun flexed its muscles across your back. Night's eyebrow crawled into the shade.

Two years later I was engaged to the tree. I wanted nothing to do with you, your demonstrative fingers, your water for the bedside. I wanted none of that comfortable silence called sleep.

And when our child came, she drew herself a lamp. She enticed insects inside, she quietly killed them.

HOUSEBOAT

One man in a cherry suit
steals my sister. Keys
conspiratorial in his pocket.
My sister a dragonfly
living on his lapel.

Telephone off the hook, I call
after them. Down the stream
they go, eating summer
like fruit, melodically
pissing under trees, a radio
tucked in the bend of their knees.

I weep in front of her empty shelves.
He has stolen her clothes. A man with a wide face
and prominent elbows. Behind him
one hag crouching in the ferns
where he will recall the light
and plug up the forest in his ears.

It is known that she wears flowers
under her arms, but my sister
is not another pink-haired
dolly. She gnaws the bone
of her book. Examines
metallic bugs on the street.
On city buses. River banks
where she left open-handed, some small
tattoo to remember
her ankle by —

In the attic a naked girl
wraps herself in a quilt.
In the basement a girl just waking.

I take my seat at the table
to the chuckle of clock and lamp.
To read a note written on a napkin in whispers.

The four winds enter through the windows,
upsetting my nightcap.
Now the dentist tells me
I am water, *Just like your mother.*
She says she will tidy my mouth.

But my teeth are a row of auditorium seats
stained with tea and honey.
They will not be loosened.
So the dentist is off to dinner
with her lover, marvelling
over the adult handwriting on the napkin.

I am only a child. There's one of us
at every bedside. In a glass
of blue foam. On a table
of someone else's making.

EVOKE

The body cannot be deceived.
It howls until held
under water. A whole city
stiff in its clothes.
Iced eyelashes of the children
who see their breath
on the other side of the window.

The lake's soul is hungry.
How often it has sat with us,
holding our hands.
At suppertime its witches are restless, unrolling
labels from soup cans.
Its children have the teeth of dogs
eating thorns in the upper balconies.

We must practice feeling empty
through the ice of imagination.
We touch empathically.
Climb innumerable stairs
to reach winter's twelve months.
We cannot disbelieve the stone
lions we croon to, never
closing our mouths.

It was during the holiday of New Thanks. Grandpère slept on the roof, on a shirt sewn with mirrors. The windows quaked, the plaster salted our plates with every snore. A ghost fogged the kitchen with prayers. The more lively dead kicked up their heels in the drafty hall as the drum kept time with its thumbs.

At dawn the humming tribe woke us: *Pick up your beds and move on.* I stuttered out of my sleeping clothes; a toothpick talisman fell from my teeth. My very good brush did not want to leave me. And my blanket wept. Where to go? I had already burned the bridges of my fingers the night before while lighting candles. I didn't know how to walk on grass without shoes.

EVERY BRIDGE A TREE

It will build your legs again,
right down from the walls,
scab upon scab.
It will melt your snow feet
and make a memory whistle
of your voice. When you come inside,
bringing your weather,
it will start the week.

For we are going to the body
and who is the boat.
Every monster of the lake
was once a king.
If washing our clothes
will give us vocabulary,
if we are thick in our skins,
bringing plants, meats and soil
across borders

as a boy changes his name to Dance.
As a girl dons her donkey skin.
The children wearing crowns
to cross the river.
Cold ever after
if we attempt to warm ourselves
with water.

CLING

Sunday it is
a chair where
a house once was.
An astrological excuse
the fiddle has for song.
For bread we had
to part with.

Now you are dead and I kiss your toes
one by one.
I hear salt,
sharply defined wind,
adolescents selling
fortune stockings
in the dark.

I will agree to being kicked
to death as the tribe
smokes in the palace.
Please tell a story
to save our lives.
White clothing disintegrating

as the disease reaches
our cardboard coffins.
Teaches the sun
one constellation.

WALKING THE OX

It refers to the small hill
behind our heart.
There is never an end
to the dancing and guitaring –
Everyone must write
a book called *House*.
Everyone must sleep
in the cannibal's mouth
and tell what his silence is,
how he never cowers
in the smell
the room belongs to.
We do not want
his orchestra. His fish
habitual as rice wine.
If we turn around
we forget four words,
three of them hallucinations,
the last another kind
of happiness, uncomfortable
but we look warmly
upon it.

BRICK OF MYTH

And you come back, good luck,
even singing,
folding your death
as it stumbles.

And we cross the cow,
jump the clock.
All forgiven on the field
where battle was
our only weather
because we couldn't tell
of another place,
how metallic the coffin tastes.

On another occasion a sparkling
young man with a heavenly eye
in the centre of his palm
clasped two canes
and I became coward,
my lambs shifting behind me.

For a spirit to enter a bottle,
there must be this –
years of words
blown to bits.

THE STOVE REFUSES TO COOL

They arrest people who stop to take pictures.
That's why my sister's spine is crooked.
Only half a piece of paper.
In October she loses her childhood notebook,
a bottle-green pair of shoes.
Those who wish to see her crutches
will have to wait.
Just as the rain teaches patience,
teeth fall from the trees.
The most experienced gravedigger
speaks softly of washing his mother.
Her room is empty because he emptied it.
He cries by the reservoir.
My sister telling him to watch
the thirty-handkerchief movie.
Naturally they are thirsty,
wanting to stir sugar in coffee.
But the country is only corn.
Themselves boarded up.
Naturally they are burning –

A BAT UNVEILED

In the museum of land mines,
my acquaintance fans her wings.
Outside the sparrows catch fire.
A tree falls to its knees.
I become the sudden murderer,
unable to recognize the radishes
of my hands.

The dictionary shudders. Again I cannot be
alone. What is left of beauty
I sop up with a napkin, believing
it a limited supply. My only reading material
gives in to the blaze.

And now I burn the legs
of the chair, lest they touch
the ground. I would give anything
for a glass of water.
But there are only dirty spoons
and a shoestring I must walk across
to reach the other corner
of the room.

I have forgotten about the beds
in the neighbouring house.
The suitcases underneath crammed with shadows.
There is a drought in my throat
when I think of them.
When I answer before they can ask.

A BRIGHTNESS BEREFT OF YOU

These words are simple people
like your grandfather.
Slap him down and he bounces back
laughing in his feathered mask.

Forget the man who devoured your father.
He's old enough to be your mother.
This girl hugging the field
while you, mere apparition on stilts,
lunge in the direction of her arms.

She kisses the postcard. Opportune lipstick.
She licks the married's cheek
in the trick of it, wearing a white gown
and glow-in-the-dark glasses.
Her lover forgets completely his primal language
for the two hours
he is under her.

Transcendent beggars, swords
weigh down their luggage.
And you a shepherd of sorts.

SEASCAPE

It never came. So I found another mother.
One with a blanket and a mouth
full of salt. I took a bag
of her to the ocean.

INTERMISSION

TWO

The spice in the wine in the mouth's
stomach. You are ever more mysterious.
A light in your throat
like amber, an almond-eyed bird
among birders.
I steal up to the attic
lest you happen to me
overnight. There I read
the leaves in a bed of my own raking.

Downstairs you shave your tic-free cheek.
Vaginally speaking, you are resplendent,
an inward castle.
But I can't be another man in the rain
holding his coat over your head.
Let's wed on the library lawn,
then kiss goodbye.

Today I drink black tea,
the gods place golden raisins
in my palm.
Today you are laughing
as you fold my image
in your wallet.

Loving is my only occupation.
It triggers the thorns in the moon.

She – a circus of roses.
Horses take her to the edge.

I – an oyster in her palm.
An eyelash on the toilet seat.
No piracy can make me more improbable.

Shallow kisses weigh down the quilt.
Light melodies precipitate war.

I am afraid to dance
for an hour and a half
with my arms in the air.

I am friend to Sagittarians
who use the word *beautiful*.

Through the blinds
light scores meridians down her body,
a canoe of sweat under her back.

I love her and I do not need to.
Better a pink shirt or the sandals
she gave away.

I stay in the bath so long I dissolve. My girlfriend drinks me. Then passes me to the toilet bowl. I swim through the sewers wearing only the dark lisp of my maiden name. I no longer own my arms and legs. When I reach the ocean, the sky stretches and does not question. I sparkle with salt and the fishes envy me my solitude.

DON'T CALL IT SANCTUARY

A brightness of birds
drawn slowly on my back
in watercolour.

Take this kiss
from the end
of my mouth
before your zodiac
steals our writhing.
I will write it
listlessly and throw
it in the river.
Over your shoulder
you are saying *never*
to everything.

You played the piano
right through your mother's death,
shuddering like candles.
Just a hint of honey
in the eyes that kept you
from becoming a pilot.
Just the scent
of it in your hair.

GRASSES

We take over the room
with our stretching. The dusk hounds
move in. A spider settles
in the centre of its web.
It is the moon to us.

We need glasses to hold
up to this light.
A common sneeze and the sudden curtsy
of farewells. Courtesy of asking
to borrow toiletries and may I have
a tarp to sleep
in the garage.

It is for you that I butter the bread
for the back door. For you
a shrine opens at each intersection.
All warmth in the eyes and arms.
For I have seen the small lizard
sunning itself on the stone in the birthroom.
In the house of the new self.

BIRTH

HAGIOGRAPHY

So frequently pitied and crossed
off the list,
now it is my turn
to forget. I remember X:
I am puzzled by this catcher of men.
Y kissing the teacher's legs.

She did advise me to take up dance
and gave a blindfold twice my age.
In the rain a word between *love* and *like*
that I had learned
as the dead woman's confidant
drowned, along with my twelve calligraphies.
The rat eating
his meal of fire
came baldly out of the grate
to meet me, white powder
on white face.

Y followed with a blanket for my escape
and some flesh from the half pear
in her palm.
Oil and vinegar breath,
her perfumed moustache.
I thought we should make use
of our bodies. Each murmur
to make us lighter.

NEW WATER

We are cutting the sea-rope.
Taking the stairs to red noise.
I pass a past life. Ounce by ounce
my feet fall asleep
at the door.

Lilacs are like that,
they root into the underworld.
A landscape of knotted silk.
No one calls it death
nor do they say it loudly.

I stand around like weather.
Bound for winter or some explicit
salt. Sheer winter.

Landscape of parts:
leaves for eyes and 'bless me' mouth.

You tremble like a patriarch.
Blind at least once a day.
Erratic like the dead.
Big, then suddenly broken,
a fingernail.

When I walk again
I will make signs
with my eternal toes.
Put food on a plate,
float it down the river.

BOXES

In stilted a cappella I sing to handsome thugs:
Make me a constellation with scissors and black paper.
The garden has no gender
but the speakers on ladders look female.
We search the house for tea, black pepper, lemon.
These keys are stubborn
statements in frost. The rooms pleasured.
Through real and fake fires
like clean characters we stroll.
Around the corner all things human.
The terrace   the sea.
But there are differences in our childhoods.
What you laugh at will make me cry.
In the graduate greenhouses
I imagine you a crow.
Your horse   your escape.
I approve but why bother.
You want to visit the ghost
you can.

A RESIDENT OF SWEET AND BITTER

I love to see a woman eating
voraciously in the street.

Now she no longer has to pretend
she drinks black tea
and is perhaps a mountain.

For I have known her body
and I can tell you:
it is a heavenly tower
you will never want to leave.

Dance with a fork and spoon, I do.
I climb the hill
to the chapel's locked gate,
take off my shirt
for the irrepressible wind,
my posture poor as the boys
who admit to kissing
in the town square.

Her second lover in the garden
licks her arm.
She turns just slightly
so you may read her profile,
see her crouching
in heels and top hat.

Creature of mud
with large shells for breasts,
a ship painted on her back.
Little girl with her chalks, her garlic,
her off-to-the-wars smile.

THE HAND IS EQUAL PARTS HEALER AND FOOL

Three suns rise —
three pears on the counter.
I don't care if you are hungry, ghost.
You don your red pants and shoes,
anxious to return to your museum.
But the house no longer shares your blanket.

Your child sneezes seven times
and opens his eyes,
reaches for bread.
I drink flowers.
We are spirits reduced to gestures.
We can be sure of nothing —

Your son and I agree,
we both saw the sun marry the sea.
Amber eyelids, a velvet curse …
We need no proof.
And this exhaustive list of wants
we can finally burn —

INSTRUMENT LIKE A DAY OF THE WEEK

The house's skin —
a study of laughter.
All the princes off to bed.
Useless, living in trees.
Barefoot and you can spank
a witch there, enjoy it
with a slice of lime.

Some drummer-angel slowly
disrobing. Noon dissolving.
We've changed but our clothes remain.

Overcast, the day
suddenly bottled.
Tide pulled back like a blanket.
Like children married
in the nurse's paintings.
Water distorts their shocked nipples.

Don't visit me, fish.
Third house with the dirt-caked books
where I gave my boy a drum.

Not knowing any better
he lived on an island.

CAUGHT READING BIOGRAPHIES IN HEAVEN

Ear to the marsh,
I knew you in the naked text.
The pre-revolutionary grammar school
where we slowed the days with thigh kisses.
It didn't interest the ashes
and it doesn't now.

You guessed the scent,
unmistakably frontal.
How my hand trembles to remember it.
Teeth. Faith.
The elders so clearly refrigerated.
And we calm.

Your feet told me they were sure
of themselves on the bribery bed.
The dream turning vulnerable
at the wrist.
Prisoners made pale in god's house.
A skeleton there and all he owns
is one dead word.
It moves up the vine in the rain.
Its rib will show you
of what we are made.
Strummed by every loss that pauses
(passes).

BEFORE THE BIRDS

Suddenly midnight, isn't it time
I took my place in unison
with the good laughter of clouds,
baby's laughter
to see the cat and dog
showing their teeth.

When we eat garlic
in a cave for one month
to answer all the rising
and falling questions,
when we spit out the river
to become the laughing dog
in the steam.

Mother gave a package of tea
and a book on palmistry,
arctic instructions
to remove the blessings
from the table, to burn the family
in their clothes.

She ate the restaurant
before turning into a pig.

I live in a watery soup
inside the huge vegetable
where ghosts wash
themselves to whiteness.
I am responsible
only for my yellow blouse.

TOWER WITH NO AUTHOR

I step into the garment buildings,
a grammar dove under my arm,
a rustle in the back of my spirit.
Seaweed dresses sway on their hangers.
My voice frills as I call
to the chicken who knows
the way up the mountain.

Honey. Peach halves.
A lesson to be learnt with matches.
The chicken knows
there is no room for my lungs
in this voluptuous shirt.
Plum chair I sit on,
the chicken crouching in my lap.
Bits of radio, a cloud: we rise
with the calmness of a boy in a tree.
He always reminds me of the rain.
A singer misplaced.
The drumbeat before it breaks off.

BIRTHDAY POEM

Out of my eyes: the good water.
For plants. Birdwash.
Whoever sits there.
After eight hours the water is new.
I make a list of things
to let go.

Whether I enslave myself
or am enslaved
by another. Fever balancing
me effortlessly, my belief
and disbelief equal.
My eyes walking.

In the year of the tiger
my father buys me
a plastic cake.
I must always wear green
and kiss him this way.
It is for us first
that he shrugged
his soldiers. His laughter
loudly and loudly.

At six his parents moved
from the farm to the sky.
I got him a baby chair and a bib
for his thirtieth.
Heavy his hat with ears,
his bigamist robe.
How little of him
is the truth, but I'm not
him yet. I'm not yet
an old woman.

A BUILDING TO BE FILLED UP WITH WATER

They leave before dawn with two fish,
two eggs and a rope smelling of pepper.

They do not walk to the mountain.
Their trousers can do that without them.
They do not take meals
on a rock in the sun.
That is for such and such a monkey.

The time of eating and sleeping is past.
Brother becomes the moon.
Sister counts her salt beads.
Every happiness in what they didn't expect.

The tiger waited with his mouth open
but they never fell from the tree.
It is so hard to keep beginning
but we have no choice.
Brother slicing the sweet apple,
man in white on the roof.

Imagine your teacher to be two people:
a table, and a fiddle from heaven.

In August the ancestors return
and we put ourselves to bed.

A STUDENT AND THE BREATH THAT HOLDS HER

We have a trouble.
A village of seeds.
Our nervous therapist in silk scarves,
a necklace of nine hundred fingers.

Sight of a man sleeping
in the mountains.
We run up the stairs.
Nobody questions our hair.
Our scarcity.
Face: shadow. Feet: clouds.

She is a student she knows lemon balm.
Why do we weep.
Brick bread. Soup of salt rock.
She shares her leaf.

At the table of zebra wood
the man naps.
He is a mountain
nothing like you'd imagine.

Not to hold the bruise
is the student's promise.
Ask her how she matches the time
in the monk's house.
How she steals the man's laughter
and hands it to us like a bowl.

ACKNOWLEDGEMENTS

Grateful acknowledgement to the editors and readers of the following publications in which some of these poems first appeared: *Carousel, CV2, The Burnside Review, eye~rhyme, The Fiddlehead, 42opus.com, Hayden's Ferry Review, No Tell Motel, The Massachusetts Review, Skein, subTerrain, Thin Air* and *2RiverView*.

'Don't Call It Sanctuary,' 'If We Are Able,' 'The Elephant Lady's Drawings,' 'Walking the Ox' and 'A Student and the Breath that Holds Her' first appeared on LOCUSPOINT: *The Place of Poetry* (locuspoint.org).

'The Hand Is Equal Parts Healer and Fool' and 'A Building To Be Filled Up with Water' were first published as part of the chapbook *ten poems/eleven years* (Breeds Like A Rumrunner, Vancouver, 2005).

The lines 'To take a pill/blue as it should be' in 'To Shrink the River' come from the writer Eljean Dodge.

'I Drink to Our Ruined House' is taken from my brother Dan's album of the same name. He stole it from Anna Akhmatova's poem 'The Last Toast.'

To any other sources I have inadvertently stolen from, my gratitude.

I wish to thank my community for sustaining me. In particular, I am indebted to the poets of vertigo west for their help with the poems in this book. Brook, Colette, Cristina, Emilie, Helen, Kim, Meliz: thank you for your kindness, humour and intelligence – and for your beautiful poems.

The eagle-eyed poet/editor Jennifer Chapis helped me to revise this book – thank you, Jenn!

Thanks also to Kevin Connolly, for his helpful edits.

My gratitude to any other friends who have read or given feedback on these poems.

Christine, this book couldn't have been written without your love and support. Thank you for your help with the poems, and for your inimitable spirit. You bring joy.

With tremendous love, I wish to thank my family. You are my teachers.

ABOUT THE AUTHOR

Jen Currin has lived in Arizona, Oregon, Massachusetts, Maine, New York and Colorado. She now makes her home in Vancouver, B.C., where she teaches creative writing. She has published one other book of poems, *The Sleep of Four Cities*.

Typeset in Joanna

Printed and bound at the Coach House on bpNichol Lane, 2008

Edited by Kevin Connolly
Designed by Alana Wilcox
Cover by Christine Leclerc
Author photo by Sarah Race

Coach House Books
401 Huron Street on bpNichol Lane
Toronto Ontario M5S 2G5

416 979 2217
800 367 6360

mail@chbooks.com
www.chbooks.com